CELLOS

by Kathryn Stevens

Published by The Child's World®
1980 Lookout Drive • Mankato, MN 56003-1705
800-599-READ • www.childsworld.com

Design element: Vector memory/Shutterstock.com
Photo credits: AGCuesta/Shutterstock.com: 21 (violin); Anton Havelaar/Shutterstock.com: 18;
Chromakey/Shutterstock.com: 21 (electric guitar); furtseff/Shutterstock.com: cover, 1, 12; nexus 7/
Shutterstock.com: 21 (lute); Peter Voronov/Shutterstock.com: 21 (harp); sbarabu/Shutterstock.com:
17; Steve Lovegrove/Shutterstock.com: 4; TheHighestQualityImages/Shutterstock.com: 21 (guitar);
Vereshchagin Dmitry/Shutterstock.com: 21 (banjo); victoras/Shutterstock.com: 11; Vladimir Melnikov/
Shutterstock.com: 8; WebCat/Shutterstock.com: 7; WHITE RABBIT83/Shutterstock.com: 14

ISBN: 9781503831872
LCCN: 2018960551

Printed in the United States of America
PA02417

Table *of* Contents

CHAPTER ONE

The Cello

People love the sound of an orchestra playing beautiful music. Cellos are an important part of an orchestra. They add a sweet, rich sound all their own.

Cellos are one kind of **stringed instrument**. Stringed instruments have strings or wires that are stretched tight. Plucking, rubbing, or tapping the strings makes a sound. Violins, guitars, and banjos are stringed instruments, too.

❮ *There are often several cellos in an orchestra.*

CHAPTER TWO

What Do Cellos Look Like?

Cellos are closely related to violins but are much, much larger. The cello's full name is the violoncello. Its body is shaped like a figure **8** or an hourglass. Attached to the body is a long **neck**. Four sturdy strings run from one end of the body all the way along the neck. A **bridge** holds the strings up off the body. The strings are wound around **tuning pegs** at the far end of the neck.

A person who plays a cello is called a cellist (CHELL-ist).

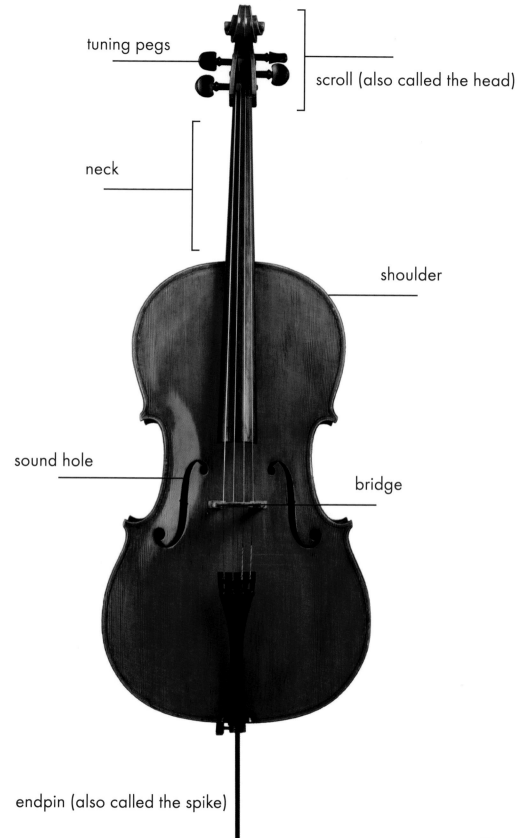

tuning pegs

scroll (also called the head)

neck

shoulder

sound hole

bridge

endpin (also called the spike)

CHAPTER THREE

How Do Cellos Make Sounds?

Try stretching a rubber band tight and then plucking it with your finger. Can you hear it make a sound? When you pluck the string, it moves rapidly back and forth, or **vibrates**. As the string vibrates, it makes a noise. Plucking or rubbing a cello's strings makes them vibrate just like the rubber band.

❮ *Most cello strings are made of metal.*

By itself, the sound of a vibrating string is not very loud. You can make it louder by holding one end against a hollow box. The box **resonates**, or vibrates along with the string. That is why cellos have such a big, hollow body. The body picks up the sound of the vibrating strings and makes it much louder. The vibrating wood of the body also helps give the cello its rich sound.

Most cellos are made of wood. Spruce and maple are often used.

You can hear a cello's vibrating strings just by plucking them. ❯

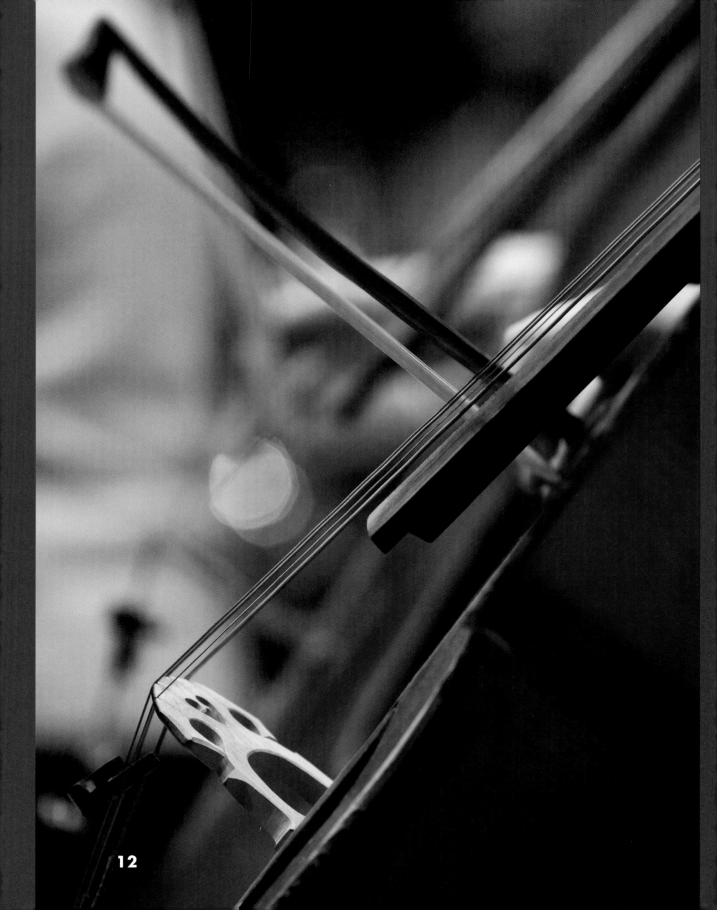

CHAPTER FOUR

Tuning a Cello

A string makes a high or low sound, or **pitch**, depending on how fast it vibrates. A short, thin, or tight string vibrates fast and produces a higher pitch. A long, thick, or loose string vibrates slowly and produces a lower pitch. Try stretching and loosening your rubber band to make higher and lower sounds. Thicker or thinner rubber bands will make different sounds, too.

❮ *The four strings on this cello are stretched tightly over the bridge.*

Each of the cello's four strings has a tuning peg to loosen it or pull it tight. Loosening the string tunes it lower. Winding it tighter tunes it higher. The strings are different thicknesses, too. The thickest string can be tuned very low. The thinner strings can be tuned higher.

Before you play a cello, you wind and loosen the strings just a little, until they sound just right. Orchestras always "tune up" that way before they play.

❮ *This cello's strings are wound around its tuning pegs.*

CHAPTER FIVE

How Do You Play a Cello?

You can play a violin by holding one end under your chin, but a cello is much too big to hold that way! Instead, you sit on a chair and hold the cello upright. A long spike keeps the cello off the floor.

One hand makes the strings vibrate by pulling a **bow** across them. This long piece of wood has hairs stretched between the ends. Rubbing the bow across the strings makes a long, steady sound. For a shorter, quicker sound, you can pluck the strings with your fingers.

Many bows are made with horsehair. The hair comes from horses' tails. ❯

While one hand makes
the strings vibrate, the other
hand presses the strings
against the neck to play
different sounds, or **notes**.
Pressing on a string shortens
the vibrating part. That
makes the string produce a higher note.

*Some players
shake their fingers
on the strings to
give long notes a
"wiggly" sound.*

Moving your fingers from one place to
another along the neck makes the cello play lots
of different notes. Good cellists can move their
fingers very fast!

❮ *Here you can see how a cello is played. The bow rubs the strings.
The cellist uses his other hand to press on the strings.*

CHAPTER SIX

The Popular Cello

Cellos have been an important part of the orchestra for many years. Some **composers** have also written music just for cellos. Some cello music is played with another instrument, such as a piano. Other pieces are for **solo** cello—a cello playing alone. Famous performers such as Pablo Casals and Yo-Yo Ma have made cellos a favorite with music-lovers all over the world.

Other Stringed Instruments

violin

lute

banjo

classical guitar

electric guitar

harp

Glossary

bow (BOH) A bow is a long piece of wood with hairs stretched between the ends. Violins and some other instruments are played by rubbing a bow across their strings.

bridge (BRIJ) On a cello, a bridge is a small, thin piece of wood that holds the strings up off the body. The bridge carries the moving strings' vibrations to the body.

composers (kum-POHZ-erz) Composers are people who write music for other people to play. Many composers have written music for cellos.

neck (NEK) The neck of a stringed instrument is the long, narrow part that sticks out from the body. A cello's four strings run all along the neck.

notes (NOHTS) Notes are musical sounds. Pressing on a cello's strings can create different notes.

pitch (PICH) In music, pitch is how high or low a sound is. In cellos, a string's pitch depends on how tight, long, or thick the string is.

resonates (REZ-uh-nayts) When something resonates, it vibrates and fills with sound. On cellos, the whole body of the instrument resonates along with the moving strings.

solo (SOH-loh) Solo means doing something alone. Some music is written for solo cello—-a single cello without any other instruments playing along.

stringed instrument (STRINGD IN-struh-ment) A stringed instrument uses strings or wires to produce its sound. Violins, guitars, and cellos are all stringed instruments.

tuning pegs (TOON-ing PEGZ) On a stringed instrument, each string is wound around a wooden or metal tuning peg. Turning the tuning peg tightens or loosens the string and changes how high or low it plays.

vibrates (VY-brayts) When something vibrates, it moves back and forth very quickly. If you pluck or rub a tightly stretched string, it vibrates and makes a sound.

To Learn More

IN THE LIBRARY

Barton, Chris. *88 Instruments*. New York, NY: Random House, 2016.

Garriel, Barbara S. *I Know a Shy Fellow Who Swallowed a Cello.* Honesdale, PA: Boyds Mills Press, 2012.

Nunn, Daniel. *Strings.* Chicago, IL: Heinemann Library, 2012.

ON THE WEB

Visit our website for links about cellos:

childsworld.com/links

Note to Parents, Teachers, and Librarians: We routinely verify our Web links to make sure they are safe and active sites. So encourage your readers to check them out!

Index

About the Author

Kathryn Stevens has an MA and a PhD in Anthropology from the University of Wisconsin-Madison, with a specialty in archaeology and environmental sciences. Kathy lives in La Crosse, Wisconsin, where she is active in archaeological research.